Never Lost © 2024 Danie

All rights reserved.

No part of this publication may be reproduced, stored in a retrieval system, or transmitted, in any form or by any means, electronic, mechanical, photocopying, recording or otherwise, without the prior written permission of the presenters.

Daniel Chelariu-Smith asserts the moral right to be identified as the author of this work.

Presentation by *BookLeaf Publishing*

Web: www.bookleafpub.com

E-mail: info@bookleafpub.com

ISBN: 9789363300439

First edition 2024

Never Lost

Daniel Chelariu-Smith

BookLeaf
Publishing

India | USA | UK

In loving memory of Grandad.

Never lost from our hearts.

ACKNOWLEDGEMENT

Always grateful to my beautiful wife and children, who make my life complete.

Never Lost

Though we wander through
Life with no map or compass
We are never lost

The Visitor

The visitor came through the patio door
Scuttled across the kitchen floor
Into the lounge, as quick as can be
Found a cosy spot, behind the settee.

As quick as he was, he wasn't unseen
As Mama announced, with a high-pitched
scream
"A mouse! A mouse!" she shrieked in fear,
"Somebody get it out of here!"

Oh, sweet little mouse, you must know it's true
This house is not a home for you!

Alerted by the cries of dismay
I hurried downstairs without a delay
Pushed all of the furniture to the side
To search for a place where a mouse might hide.

Under the table? Behind the curtain?
"He's in there somewhere!" Mama was certain
In the cabinet? Beneath the chair?
I couldn't find him anywhere.

Oh, sweet little mouse, you must know it's true
This house is not a home for you!

Then all of a sudden, looking at me
The beadiest eyes that I ever did see
Sparkling brightly, whiskers a-twitching
With a helpless expression, I found somewhat
bewitching.

"Oh, isn't he cute!" without thought, I declared
But this was a view that was not widely shared
So, I reached down to gather him up with great
care
But that sweet little creature was no longer
there!

Oh, sweet little mouse, you must know it's true
This house is not a home for you!

My chance had expired – I knew it was so
He was looking right at me, but I let him go
My compassionate smile quickly changed to a
frown
As I turned the living room upside-down.

Alas, it was useless, for hard as I sought
My friend made it clear that he wouldn't be
caught
For vain was my search and helpless my plight
Not a squeak, not a rustle, not a whisker in sight.

Oh, sweet little mouse, you must know it's true
This house is not a home for you!

By now Mama's panic had begun to subside
So, she sprang into action and went for a ride
To seek out a shop that would hopefully sell
A trap for the mouse (and some mouse treats as
well)

It was barely ten minutes that I had to wait
Till Mama returned with some mouse traps and
bait
We set them out quickly and waited to see
What the outcome for our little house guest
would be.

Oh, sweet little mouse, you must know it's true
This house is not a home for you!

The hours passed by, and the day turned to night
We retired to bed, and we switched out the light
I drifted to sleep, with one thought on my mind:
'When I woke in the morning, what would I
find?'

But I woke in the night to a clattering sound
Jumped out of bed, darted downstairs and found
In a trap, peering out, with a look of dismay
The sweet little pest I'd been chasing all day.

Oh, sweet little mouse, you must know it's true
This house is not a home for you!

I went to the garden to set my friend free
And I swear for a second, he looked back at me
Gave a twitch of his whispers, mischievously
smiled
Then scampered off happily, back to the wild.

Stop!

Stop!

Even though life is hurtling
Towards oblivion
Or perhaps simply
Some untold form of chaos
Still, you must

Stop!

Even though your days are full
Of great responsibility
And duties that would gladly
Consume every waking hour
Still, you must

Stop!

Even when your life, it seems
Has spun out of control
And you no longer
Hold the key to your own destiny
Still, you must

Stop!

Even when the daily news
Tells gruesome tales
Of society in turmoil
Lurching mindlessly towards destruction
Still, you must

Stop!

Even though your restless nights
Are punctuated by desperate visions
Of a fearful future
That leave you wearily trudging
Through endless days
Still, you must

Stop!

For it is only when you stop
That you can truly find
The strength within
To keep moving
Onward

Amelia, Sweetie

Amelia, Sweetie
Look at you now!
A charming young lady
An infant no longer
Beautiful, confident
Your own sense of style
And every day
Growing wiser and stronger

Amelia, Sweetie
Open your eyes
To adventure and treasure
That waits to be found
Choose happiness daily
Enjoy every moment
With your heart in the stars
But your feet on the ground

Amelia Sweetie
Our lioness
With a heart that is brave
And a roar that is true
Hold love in your heart
As you stride forth each day
And remember your pride
Will be standing by you

Colour me in

Life in black and white
Till you appeared, full of love
And coloured me in

I'll Start my Diet Tomorrow

I'll start my diet tomorrow
Just one more takeaway for me
A pizza, some wine and a little dessert
Ice-cream probably

Yes, starting from tomorrow
I'll count my calories with care
I've prepped my lunches for the week
My 'sweet treat' shelf's completely bare

The fridge is loaded up with veg
The fruit bowl's overflowing
I've even set a weblog up
To chart how it's all going

I've downloaded the best new app
To track my food intake
I'll log my meals quite honestly
(Unless I have a slice of cake)

I'll exercise tomorrow
Of that you can be sure
My fitness regime, the strictest by far
Of any I've done before

I'll start my diet tomorrow
Might even join a group
I'll win awards and won't get bored
Of only eating soup

I've been looking in the mirror
And it's time to get it right
(The button popped off my new jeans
And all my shirts feel tight)

And if I start tomorrow
I'll be slim for Christmas Day
Providing there aren't too many
Slip-ups along the way

I'll start my diet tomorrow
But first just one more little treat
Savouring each precious bite
Of things I actually like to eat

I'll start my diet tomorrow
With a sense of déjà vu
Last time I lasted just one day
Perhaps this time I'll manage two!

Heart Filled with Love

Gently rocking
Her newborn child
In tired arms
She marvels at the beauty of the universe
Wrapped up in a helpless infant
Her heart filled with love

Gently resting
Her head upon his shoulders
She gazes into deep blue eyes
Reflecting love
As he pulls her close
His heart filled with passion

Gently guiding
Her feet down the aisle
He turns and wonders at her perfection
Squeezing her hand before letting it go
Passed on to another forever
His heart filled with pride

Gently touching
His fragile, broken skin
Weathered by many long years
She holds back the tears
To bravely kiss him goodbye
Her heart filled with sorrow

Gently breathing
Cherishing his final moments
He feels the warm touch of loving lips
As surrounded by love
He drifts into eternal sleep
His heart filled with peace

Five Years of Us

Five years of me and you
Five years of you and me
Five years of perfect happiness and blissful
harmony
1,826 days walking by your side
60 months travelling this rollercoaster ride.

Five years of me and you
Five years of you and me
Five great years of laughs and tears and making
memories
260 weeks of adventuring and fun
48,824 hours of the journey we've begun.

Five years of me and you
Five years of you and me
Five years of gently building up our precious
family
520 weekend days exploring life together
2,629,440 moments – the beginning of forever.

Five years of me and you
Five years of you and me
Five years of settling down at night and holding
you closely
Half a decade, hand-in-hand, under the
moonlight
157,766,400 seconds of loving you and kissing
you goodnight.

Footnotes:
i. This poem can be personalised by substituting
the initials of your name and that of your loved
one, for example, "five years of D and M, five
years of M and D".
ii. This only works if either you or your partner
have an initial that rhymes with 'me' or 'you'.
This accounts for approximately half of the
possible letter combinations, according to my
calculations, but is unfortunate if your names
are, for example, Amy and Matthew.
iii. If your name is Zachary, you will need to
pronounce Z the American way.
iv. Although W does technically rhyme with
'you,' it's a bit of a stretch to pronounce and
significantly disrupts the rhythm of the poem.
Sorry, Williams and Wendys.

v. This poem can also be personalised for the number of years that you've been together, of course, though you may need a calculator.
vi. This poem is an excellent illustration of why large numbers are seldom used in poetry.

Not Every Day

Not every day will be
A perfect, vibrant symphony
With boundless joy and happiness
Enrobed in ecstasy;
Some days, they may be grey
And darling, that's okay
Just fix your eyes on distant lights
And dreams that guide your way.

Not every travelled mile
Will be with verve and style
Not every passerby you meet
Will greet you with a smile;
For some paths will be rough
Some journeys will be tough
Look deep within and you will find
My angel, you're enough.

Not every sky, it's true
Will be a dazzling blue
Bright sunshine beating boldly down
And not a cloud in view;
For sometimes storms abound
Dark shadows gather round
Take heart, my dear, and never fear
For silver linings can be found.

Spirit of Adventure

The true spirit of adventure
Lies deep within the soul
And can never be tamed

Telenovela

Pablo and Rosita
Shared a secret kiss last night
But Matteo walked in on them
And he and Pablo had a fight

Rosita slipping out the back
Was kidnapped by Benito's men
Leaving Pablo wondering if
He'd ever see his girl again

Down the street Francesca weeps
She's misplaced her engagement ring
She took it off to clean the house
And now can't find that precious bling

Ernesto's in some trouble too
He's got involved with local thugs
First, they had him smuggling booze
And now they're moving on to drugs

Pascal's in the hospital
It seems he crashed that jeep of his
He's suffering from amnesia
And can't remember who he is

Perhaps he didn't crash at all
And someone drove him off the road
But who could want poor Pascal dead?
And who knows where his jeep's been towed?

Yet what an opportunity
For Quinn, who's sitting at his side
She's taken over Pascal's ranch
And all the staff are terrified

She's making changes left and right
Which in itself is rather strange
She used to be a quiet girl
But now it seems she's changed

And if you look quite close enough
There's something different in her face
It isn't really Quinn at all!
Her evil twin's usurped her place!

In Freddie's mansion, out of town
Something doesn't feel quite right
His wife Perdita's acting strange
And sneaking out on Friday night

Will she get away with it?
Or is she going to be betrayed
For following her, a few steps back
Is Betsy, her suspicious maid

She trails her to a parking lot
A shady figure greets her there
It's Fergus, Freddie's brother
For they're having an affair

Suddenly a light comes on
Someone else is here as well
But…
We'll have to wait to find out who
The music starts to swell

That's pretty much what happened
On our mother's TV show today
But wait, stay tuned, there's more to come
For Episode 2 is on the way!

Poisoned Spiteful Words

Poisoned spiteful words
Spat by the flickering, forked tongues
Of those who could never know
What it's like to live your life
Never bore your burden
Nor wore your shoes
Yet carry those fiery pitchforks of judgement

What would they do
If they truly knew
How easily these thorns
Could disrupt
The fragility of your life?
Would they bury their heads in shame
Or brandish their barbs just the same?

Yet too late they will see
That your life and theirs
Are intertwined eternally
For no more can they take back those words
Than you can retake your life
Stolen so easily
By poisoned, spiteful words

Silently Drowning

silently drowning
in worry and care
seeking salvation
from anywhere
days seem to darken
filled with despair
nights getting longer
slumber so rare
secretly hoping
for someone to share
this burden, but finding
nobody there
look to the heavens
unanswered prayer
last hope dissolving
lost in the air

On Our Wedding Day

On our wedding day
The guests arrived from near and far
Some by taxi, some by car
Most headed quickly for the bar
(For we'd agreed to pay!)
On our wedding day

On our wedding day
The sun shone bright, and the sky was blue
With not a single cloud in view
A metaphor for my life with you
As events got underway
On our wedding day

On our wedding day
I stood in the sun, and watched you appear
Holding my breath as you drew near
We read our vows, and I held back a tear
As I heard the words you chose to say
On our wedding day

On our wedding day,
We ran up the aisle to a perfect song
Then the stars came out and the wine was strong
And we danced together all night long
When our tunes began to play
On our wedding day

On our wedding day
The night drew in and the music died
I went to bed with you by my side
A happy groom with his perfect bride
A memory forever to stay
On our wedding day

In the Fog

In the fog I am safe
Enrapt in its warm embrace
Enclosed by its tender care
Nothing can harm me there.

In the fog I am secure
A thick wall of silence that makes me sure
A blanket of infinite size
That hides me from prying eyes.

In the fog I feel no harm
Surrounded by its misty charm
Safely, softly it holds me tight
Protects me from the darkest night.

A Mother's Day Ditty

Mama, we love you
You really are the best
You're lovely in your smart work clothes
Or in your pants and vest
You care for us each day and night
And most of the time you get it right
True, no one's perfect – but you're the closest
We all love you
The absolute mostest!
You make us laugh
You make us smile
You always go the extra mile
To bring the sunshine to our days
And light up our lives
In so many ways
So, thank you Mama
From the bottom of our hearts
You don't tell us off for our burps and farts
You try to understand what's in our heads
And you tuck us up all snuggly in our beds
So today we want to thank you
With this little rhyme
We love you
Times infinity
Until the end of time!

The Apocalypse Cometh

The apocalypse cometh
And I think that I'm ready
Got tinned food in the garage a plenty
I've worked out the rations
And there's surely enough
To survive 15 years, maybe 20.

Got a small rack of weapons
Carefully selected
To fight off the zombie hordes
And a special collection
Of things I can trade with
Alien overlords.

Down in my basement
I've crafted a bunker
In case we go radioactive
It is safe and secure
With an O2 supply
And a treadmill so I can stay active.

The apocalypse cometh
And I *was* feeling ready
Preparing for every disaster
Till this morning my sister
Brought her kids to my house
And left them for me to look after!

Summer Lolidays!

"School's out!"
The children shout
Summer holidays are here
Best time of the year
(Except Christmas maybe,
It's undecided)
Never mind,
Don't get sidetracked
Gotta get packed

Just one day
To pack and prepare
Mum's got washing
Everywhere
Wash the clothes
Dry the clothes
Iron the clothes
Pack
(She'll do it all again
When we get back)

Dad's in the garage
Less frantic
More steady
Getting the transportation ready
Tyres checked
Oil checked
Engine humming perfectly
Screen wash filled
Boot cleared out
Got details for the RAC
(Let's hope we don't need them!)
All fueled up and ready to go
Back inside for a cup of joe,
(Or tea, maybe)

Children stay
Out the way
Quietly play
They'll be okay
It's just one day

Bedtime comes
Bedtime for some
Still a few jobs for Dad and Mum
Gotta be done
Soon they too
Drop into bed
Busy day behind
Busy day ahead

Alarm rings
Dad springs
Out of bed, soon brings
Steaming coffee to his wife
The elixir of life
Can't start the day without it
(So she says)
They go their separate ways

Dad to the kitchen
Mum upstairs
"Happy Holidays!"
She declares
Get the kids
Out of bed
(Eldest one's a sleepy head)
Washed and dressed
Holiday clothes
Pack the toys
And books they've chose
Grab some breakfast
Juice and toast
Are we ready?
Almost
Head downstairs
Shoes on
Where has the time gone?

Dad makes sandwiches
Cheese and ham
Except for the little one
Only eats jam —
White bread, crusts off,
(Dad's getting soft)
Next, he packs
Journey snacks
A good selection
(the sugary kind)
Add some fruit
Crisps too
No food left behind!

Final job:
Pack the car
Toughest task so far
No doubt
Kids help out
Dragging baggage all about
Will it fit?
Dad's on it
Place them right
Squeeze it tight
No problem!
Soon done
(Played Tetris when he was young!)

Time to go
Everyone set?
What did we forget?
Charger?
Check
Toothbrush?
Check
Swimming costumes?
Check
Got the raincoats
In the car
In case it's wet
(It is the UK after all
One can never be too sure!)

Great work!
Almost done
Last toilets everyone!

Leave house
Lock door
Pile in
Belts on
Say a prayer
Start engine
Off we go!

(Only 40 minutes later
than we planned to leave
A new record, I believe!)

Gotta drive
Pretty far
Several hours
In the car
First few —
Happy days!
Traffic lights
All go our way
Music plays
Keep us grooving
No queueing
Keep on moving
Until…

"Guys, I need the toilet!"
"10 minutes to the next service station
Can you hold it?"
"I'll try!"

Stop for a toilet break
A coffee and a cake
Sun is shining
Feeling fine
We'll be there
In no time

Back in the car
Back on the road

Oh no!
Traffic's slowed!

Bumper to bumper
Crawling along
Try to find an upbeat song
Wind down the windows
Get some air
Horns beeping
Everywhere
At a standstill
Impatiently waiting
Some drivers out
Investigating

Sirens wail
Police are here
Won't be long before it's clear

Moving again
Now we're cooking!
Out the windows
Everyone looking
Scenery's changing
Lots of green
Hardly a building
To be seen
Round the next corner
Will it be?
Yes!
"I can see the sea!"

Park car
Not too far
To the beach…

Oh no!
We forgot the picnic blanket!

Quick stop
Beach shop
Problem gone, moving on…

Short trek to the beach
Phone signal out of reach
Two weeks of peace
Finally, has begun
Mum's stretching out
In the sun
Kids close by
Having fun
Playing in the sand
Castle planned
Bucket and spade in hand

Dad's in the chair with a book and a beer
Summer holidays are here!

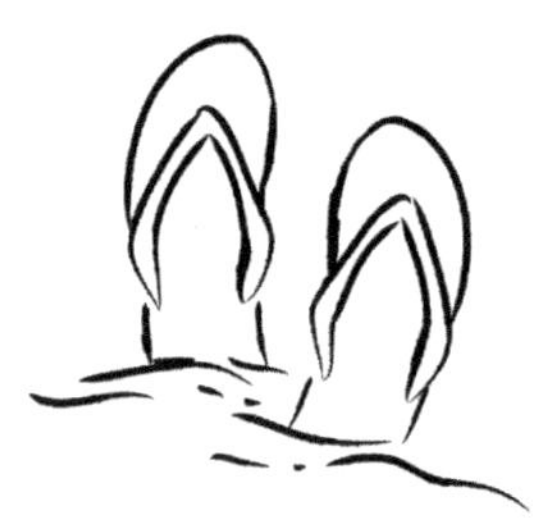

Two Hearts

two hearts intertwined
one forever, yours and mine
bound by love alone

One Drop of Sunshine

One drop of sunshine
Is all I need
For love to grow
My heart to feed
For the darkest night
To turn to day
And banish
These dark clouds away

One drop of sunshine
'Tis enough
When days are dreary
When the path is rough
To pick me up
When I've been cast down
To rescue me
As I start to drown

One drop of sunshine
Brings me life
One ray of joy
Dispersing strife
Where shadows lurked
The light breaks through
Delivers warmth
And bliss anew

Choices

Choose to be happy
Choose each day to be content
Choose a life of love

A Twist in the Tail

You might recall a solemn tale
That I did previously regale
(If you don't then take a look:
It's number two within this book!)

It was the story of a mouse
Who ventured deep inside our house
That story ended happily
But that's not quite the end, you see.

For after that surreal event
We felt that it was time we went
Down to the pet store, and brought back
A perfect, playful, little cat!

Our Toffee

Our Toffee
Ginger and white
Out in the garden
Likes to fight
Terrorizes
The local cats
We're not too proud
Of that.

Our Toffee
Brought home a frog
3 mice and a bird
The whole catalogue
Thinks he's bringing
Us a treat
Oh…
How sweet!

Our Toffee
Big and strong
Runs away
When he's done wrong
Soon returns
Whimpering
Can't stay mad
At him.

Our Toffee
Sleeps in a ball
Doesn't seem big or tough
At all
Rests on our legs
The whole night through
Our Toffee,
We love you!

The Dice Decide

When life gets tough,
Becomes too much
I let the dice decide
Don't make a choice
Can't get it wrong
If luck is on your side.

And if it's not
Then who's to fault?
At least I'm not to blame
The cards are dealt
I'll take my hand
And let fate play its game.

Sometimes the way
Is clear as day
The pathway marked with lights
But when it's not
I sacrifice
Decision-making rights.

Good fortune rests
Her loving smile
Upon the brave they say
And who could be
More brave than I
To live my life this way?

When providence
Cannot make sense
Of this old life of mine
What choice remains
But live my days
Without a grand design?

If destiny
Won't rescue me
I guess that is my lot
But if the dice
Have to decide
It means that I do not.

Success

For years I struggled
Only to find the secret:
Make better choices

Happy Wife, Happy Life

Happy wife, happy life
Happy me, with you beside
Every day a precious gift
With my perfect, gentle bride.

Happy days, here to stay
Happy moments spent together
Making every second count
Drenched in happiness forever.

You Are Miles

You are strong, you are tall
You've got mad skills on the ball
You brave, you are wild
You are Miles

You are smart, you are cool
You've been working hard at school
You're a star, you'll go far
You are Miles

You are thoughtful, you are kind
You've a fascinating mind
You are caring, good at sharing
You are Miles

You collect Match Attax
And amaze us with strange facts
You play games like a pro
You are Miles

You are funny and engaging
Your vocabulary's amazing
You make friends where'er you go
You are Miles

You've got rhythm, you can rhyme
Hear you singing all the time
Play your tunes, rock the rooms
You are Miles

You ride bikes, you wear jeans
And you jump on trampolines
You are smooth, you've got style
You are Miles

You can read, you can write
Always stay up late at night
You like books, movies too
You are Miles

You're polite when we're out
Make us proud, without a doubt
You're our mate, you are great
You are Miles

You send sadness away
Give us cuddles every day
You are loved, you are ours
You are Miles

Glass

Though you see in me
Confidence, my mind remains
As fragile as glass

Pray What Foul Wounds

Pray what foul wounds she lays across my chest
That I should bleed more deeply than the sea
And yet in bleeding, I am truly blessed
My heart now holds a little less of me

Redemptive whispers echo in my mind
Diverting me from any earthly thought
And in such musings, truth must be divined
That renders mine own pertinence as nought

Her hand conceals the weapons that will steal
My final breath and thus I comprehend
Such knowledge that she only can reveal
Now broken and forsaken, I can mend

And thus, my final destiny is sealed
For resting in her arms, I will be healed

I do not Seek

I do not seek a lot in life
No plans by greed applied
A place that I can call my home
With loved ones by my side
Health, happiness, and harmony
Are all that I desire
And maybe one romantic spark
To set my heart on fire

My Masterpiece

I'm working on my masterpiece
Painting strokes with care
Producing my own work of art
That I'll be proud to share

I etch each line with love and thought
Working every day and night
Mix colours conscientiously
To get each shade just right

I'll pay special attention to
My characters' interaction
I'll edit their expressions 'till
They're formed to satisfaction

And even when my tools are down
I keep these images in mind
Each element mapped out to be
Painstakingly defined

My artistic interpretations
Will be clear for all to see
Declaring proudly to the world
There's only one of me

This canvas is uniquely mine
A single page that I must fill
I'll rectify mistakes I make
Developing my craft and skill

My magnum opus fills my days
Yet every touch holds unknown worth
For it's the story of the path
I walk while here on planet Earth

And when I take my final breath
And lay this mortal frame to rest
My masterpiece so beautiful
Will tell you I was truly blessed

Haiku #7

Death separates us
An opaque veil that once crossed
Can no more be passed

Music Days

5 am alarm sounds
Plays a random song
Try to recognise that tune
So I can sing along
Intro sounds familiar
Sure I've heard it plenty
Suddenly the beat kicks in
Of course, it's Matchbox…

Twenty minutes later,
Singing in the shower
Water splashing down on me
Cleansing me with power
Got my favourite playlist on
Drench the room with soul
Suddenly it mellows out
The legend, Nat King…

Cold September morning
Driving in my car
Just time for a couple songs
Office isn't far
Journey's pretty smooth today
Traffic all but dead
Creep into the parking lot
Enjoying Radio…

Head up to my office
Wearing my work face
Listen to that soft work hum
No music in this place
Pop my trusty earbuds in
Helps the time to pass
Check my e-mails listening to
A touch of Super…

"Gracias Monsignor"
Smiles the young barista
She winks at me across the room
Not sure I can resist her
Focus on the music
Washing over me
Some Tina Turner power pop
Remixed by Warren…

Gee, this morning's dragging!
Will it ever end?
Check my phone for messages
Got one from my friend
Shares some news from 'Bands in Town'
This one might be fun
Haven't seen them live for years
Let's go see Silver…

Sun is shining brightly now
Heading off to lunch
Brought a tasty sandwich
And a pack of Monster Munch
In the cafeteria
Music starts to play
Enjoy my lunch while breathing in
The tones of David…

Graham from accounting
Wants a quick update
He's looming over my workspace
Getting quite irate
Suddenly his phone rings
The dark clouds start to lift
His ringtone (quite surprisingly)
Is 'Stay' by Taylor…

Swiftly heading out the door
Working day is done
Finally, I'm heading home
'Neath the setting sun
Sky is slowly turning red
Ethereal and pretty
My workday ire soon drifts away
Thanks to Owl…

City lights are twinkling now
As the night draws in
Pull the curtains, settle down
With a glass of gin
Select a CD from the shelf
Glad to be alive
End the day by dancing round
To 'ABC' by Jackson…

Gentle Regret

Gentle regret
Softly tugs upon my mind
A fractional weight on my heart each day
Things that might have been
Things I left behind

Blissful Delicate Repose

Blissful, delicate repose
Captured for a moment in between
The waking world and some beguiling dream
No consciousness of time or space remains
Gently drift o'er ethereal planes
Be still my heart and join me for a while
Where weary souls can draw a breath and smile
Enjoy the perfect peace reserved for those
Who enter blissful, delicate repose

Alisha Writes Stories

Alisha writes stories
Daryl is an actor
Benny is a judge on Romanian X-factor

Andy's a policeman
Tony races cars
Suzy owns a chain of rather fancy bars

David works in politics
Giles produces beer
Betty is a meatball chef, working for Ikea

Lucy runs a corner shop
Stuey's in construction
Olga's the director of a touring kids' production

Luka joined the army
Joshua's a preacher
Abigail just recently became a headteacher

Bobby won the lottery
And brought a stately home
Theresa is an air hostess – she always loved to
roam

Timmy has a YouTube show
With twenty thousand likes
Tyler travels round to schools fixing up kids'
bikes

Stavros is a caretaker
Mario's a plumber
Larissa was a lifeguard – but only through the
summer

Sandy is a dentist
Fixing people's smiles
Eldrick runs a charity that rescues crocodiles
(and the occasional alligator, I'm reliably
informed)

Ken delivers takeaways
Geoff's a flying doctor
Sue became a therapist 'cause nothing ever
shocked her

Suki is a wedding planner
Barney is a miner
Kimberley dropped out of school to be a game
designer

Johnny is a carpenter
Gail became a lawyer
Kerry is an agent for a secretive employer

Alfie is a postal worker
Jen's a ballerina
Matthew left his other job to be a
window-cleaner

Kevin is a llama farmer
Jane is a detective
Gerry's a consultant making systems more
effective

Delroy is an engineer
Emma is a stylist
Monty's a celebrity, moving up the Y-list!

Alan is an astronaut
Rob sells mobile phones
Anne's an archaeologist like Indiana Jones

And me?

I write poems!

I Write Poems

I got no use for paragraphs
'Cause I write poems
And sentences just waste my time
When all I wanna do is rhyme

Droppin' words onto a page
That don't need to take an age
Proofreading? Nah, not for me
'Cause when I'm writing, I am free!

I try a thousand different words
Just to make my message clear
Might even try to catch your ears
With onomatopoeia

I use devices regularly
Just like pathetic fallacy
For when I write my poetry
The sun is smiling down on me

Alliteration is my friend
And metaphors I can extend
They give my words new lease of life
While similes cut like a knife

Verses, stanzas – that's my game
You see I ain't no amateur
Can even knock a sonnet up
In iambic pentameter
(I know this 'cause they teach Shakespeare in
school!)

I'll write a tanka, write an ode
I'll even write a villanelle
I'll turn my pen to any form
And usually do it well

Like everyone, I have my flaws
I tend to mix my metaphors
I try too hard to make lines rhyme
And get my beats wrong all the time

My sentence structures fluctuate
I don't take time to punctuate
My rhyme schemes change from verse to verse
But frankly I could do much worse

And…
When I write Haiku
With the syllables spot on
I sometimes get it wrong!

Never mind, I don't give in
The words just come from deep within
For this is my vocation
I'm a poetry sensation!
(And the king of procrastination…
Which is probably why I write poems in the first
place!)

And what would be the point of me
If I could not write poetry?
I know not what else I could be
Without my dose of vitamin P

Not everyone will think me cool
I don't write for the kids at school
I got no rizz – that's what they say
I-Y-K-Y-K…

But poetry helps me express
The thoughts and feelings in my mind
And when I write creatively
It sets my spirit free, I find

And poetry comes from the heart
'Cause that's the perfect place to start
So everybody join with me
Let's give it up for poetry!

Game Over

Humanity has reached the end
Has tore itself apart
Too many years of bickering
Corroding its own heart

For toxic words and poisoned thoughts
Have terrorised its soul
We've reached the point of no return
Too late to make it whole

Too many people out to harm
So quickly to attack
And words once spoken out of spite
Can ne'er be taken back

The world was ours to tend and yet
We failed it without measure
And drained the very lifeblood from
This rare terrestrial treasure

We've scarred the land with many wars
Created air pollution
With plastics littered precious seas
And sought out no solution

A small minority remains
Of poets, thinkers, lovers
Too few to make a difference now
And save Earth from the others

Now sad, but true, all hope is lost
The damage has been done
We've lost ourselves, destroyed our home
Our death march has begun

Tanka #2

Perchance we may find
When we die, we leave behind
Only what is kind
Would we follow this same path
Marked by bitterness and wrath?

Never Found

Some things once lost are never found
Gone without a trace
Destined to exist in some
Eternal hiding place

Though once held dear, they now reside
Without an earthly home
And endless searching never could
Discover where they roam

Some things once lost leave aching wounds
Their value has no measure
So, heed this warning now my friend,
Take care of what you treasure

September Sonnet

Oh summertime, I bid you fond farewell
As wearily to work I must return
The end of hazy, lazy summer nights
Marshmallows toasting as the campfires burn

Alarm clocks break my slumber once again
A death knell filling aching heart with dread
I've cast my shorts and t-shirts to the side
Now suits and ties adorn my corpse instead

Bright flowers, sunshine fade into the past
The colour in my life returns to grey
My mellow coffee mornings soon replaced
Commuting on a busy motorway

Farewell to summer holidays, my friend
For even perfect things come to an end.

Croque Monsieur

Today I'm making croque monsieur
(Or ham and cheese toasty, if you prefer)
I'm using up some leftovers
Two types of cheese – how cordon bleu!
A tomato, bread, and a packet of ham
Well, half a packet – about 80 gram.

I smear some butter on the bread
(It's actually a plant-based spread)
Then chop things up with expert flair
Tomato squirting everywhere
(I can't find my serrated knife, you see)

I tear the ham up into pieces
And lay them out upon the cheeses
Close it up, like a proper baker
Then throw it in the toasty-maker

(At this point, I do a few dishes and pour myself
a glass of slightly flat lemonade)

Soon the bread turns golden brown
The time has come to wolf it down
Sandwich ready, table laid
My final meal before I'm paid

For today's the last day of the month
And I'm having croque monsieur for lunch.

And If We Fall

And if we fall
Will there be
Another opportunity
To find the light?
A chance to make it right?

And if we fall
Is that the end?
No way to ever
Make amends?
To start over again?

And if we fall,
Will we be through?
The final rites
For me and you?
No future hope in sight?

We fell before, but fall again?
Some things we cannot mend.

No. 44

Though we live our lives with synthetic pride
And attempt to present as dignified
One truth can never be denied
Everyone has something to hide.

The Fate of Many Bananas

I brought some green bananas
From the local market stall
But the colour didn't stay the same
For very long at all.

They quickly changed to yellow
As ripe as ripe could be
And I gobbled some bananas up
Two, or maybe three.

Now just a few days later
They've turned to brown instead
So, I find myself back here again
Baking banana bread!

Heartbreak

The shards of my heart
Lie scattered across the room
Where once you were mine

The Junk Shop

The junk shop is a wondrous place
I visit when I'm bored
I stroll around its passageways,
Explore its precious hoard.

It's always full of friendly folk
Just looking for a gem
(Though it gets a little feisty
If you want the same as them!)

Each nook and cranny overflows
With treasures never sought
I've visited a thousand times
And this is what I've bought…

A briefcase
A suitcase
A pencil case too
A bookcase
A shoelace
A seat for the loo

A large canvas print of a street scene in Rome
A plaque for the kitchen that reads 'Home Sweet
Home'

A poster
A scooter
A classic Gameboy
A model of a spitfire and
A superhero toy

Not to mention…

A garden gate
Some fishing bait
A wooden box for my magic tricks
A coffee mate
A wooden crate
An antique game of pick-up sticks

A chest of drawers
A pair of oars
An ornate vase my wife adores
Two painted doors
Some petit fours
And several famous music scores

A telescope,
A microscope
A vintage kids' kaleidoscope
A periscope
A bar of soap
An unused hank of cotton rope

An old canoe
A didgeridoo
A doll's house and a box of hooks
A green guitar
A scimitar
A pet mouse and a set of books
(Encyclopaedia, actually)

A wheelchair ramp
A parking clamp
A working rusty Davy lamp
A book of stamps
Two guitar amps
A workbench with a bright blue clamp

Some old cigars
Some matchbox cars
Some vinyl for my record player
A cuckoo clock
A butcher's block
A VHS of Dragonslayer

(Though I'm still on the lookout for a VHS
player if anyone sees one…)

The junk shop is a special place
With bargains guaranteed
A modern-day Aladdin's cave
Of things I never knew I'd need!

Dougie Draws Dinosaurs

Dougie draws dinosaurs
Freddie's friends with frogs
Evie eats enormous eggs
Lyla lectures logs

Miles makes masks for monkeys
Amelia avoids altercations
Ottie orders olive oil
Vesper values vaccinations

(At this point I'm just glad there are
No boys in our family named Xavier!)

To Whom it may Concern

Dear Madam or Sir,

I'm sure you'll concur,
This whole situation is quite out of hand

By whom was this planned?
And why should we stand
For constant disruption wherever we go?

And surely you know
Your progress is slow
For me and my family are far from alone

In having a moan
And making it known
That we'd like some action to move things along

Our feelings are strong
It's really quite wrong
That you're setting up roadworks all over this
town

It's slowing us down
And making us frown
And we'd like you to tell us for how long and
why?
I await your reply

Sincerely,
Goodbye

The Lost Sock

The lost sock
Could not be found
Though Mama hunted
All around
The latest victim
Of the washing machine
Lost and gone
But most likely clean!

All Beautiful

Your smile
creates a spark
in my undivided heart

Your touch
washes pleasure
down my spine

Your voice gently
soothes my soul
in life's stormy sea

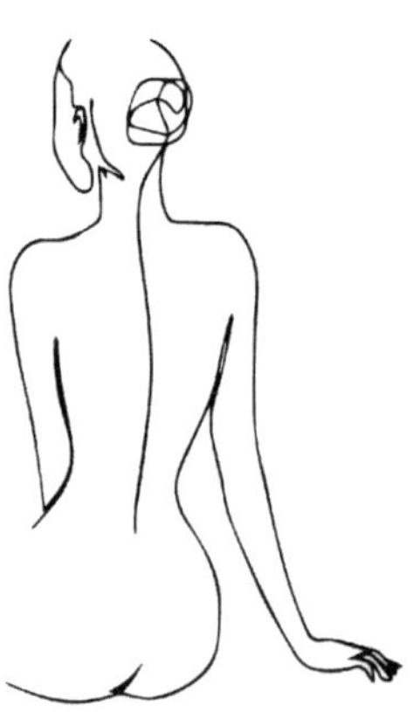

Your embrace
reassures me
you are mine

Your kisses
set a fire
that consumes
me to the core

Your fragrance
tears my mind
out of control

Your breath
whispers sweetly
to my spirit,
notes of joy

Your love
wraps around
my very soul

My dear,
you are all
beautiful

And Then We Dance

Sometimes life gets heavy,
Enough to wear us down
Sometimes smiles are hard to find
And every muscle wants to frown
Sometimes we can't help but feel
Trapped by circumstance
And then we dance

Sometimes there's a darkness that
Replaces all our light
Sometimes though we try our best
We just can't get it right
Sometimes life can let us down
Because we took a chance
And then we dance

Sometimes shadows overwhelm
All hopes of happiness
Sometimes we are scathed by thoughts
We never would confess
Sometimes it can feel like
We are living in a trance
And then we dance

Sometimes we may stumble
The skies grow gloomy grey
Sometimes we may wander from
The lights that guide our way
Sometimes we may find ourselves
Lost in the expanse
And then we dance

Sometimes rays break through the clouds
And shine a little light
Sometimes there's a crack of dawn
Within an endless night
Sometimes there's a glimmering
Of happiness perchance
And then we dance

No Refunds

No refunds, no reruns
Only one chance
One beautiful story
One intricate dance

No cut scenes, no call-backs
Just the one show
One flawless performance
One perfect tableau

No shortcuts no 'next bus'
One ticket to ride
One journey to savour
And finish with pride

This Mortal Labyrinth

To find safe passage
Through this mortal labyrinth
Let love be your guide

Letting Go

Letting go
Is hard to do
Relinquishing control
Giving it to you

No longer ruled
By my demands
My destiny
Is in your hands

You hold the key
My hands are bare
For you could take me
Anywhere

My life now feels
Incomplete
Sitting in
The passenger seat!

You Were Mine

You were dazzling, full of life
Bright and blissful as sunshine
You were spirited and warm
And you were mine

You spoke true words from your heart
Your soft lips a sweet red wine
Like a river your love flowed
And you were mine

You were gentle, you were mild
Your soul delicate and fine
Every touch would make you smile
And you were mine

Sparkling eyes like burning stars
Tender kisses so divine
Beauty far beyond compare
And you were mine

It was perfect for a while
But our paths did not align
Now a memory from a dream
And you were mine

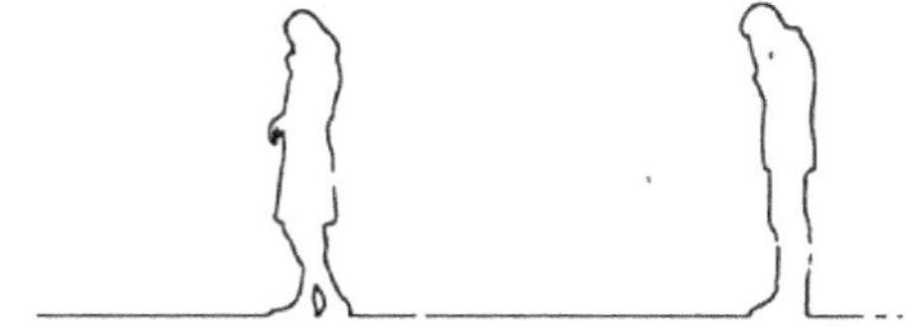

Early Autumn Shades

Early autumn shades
Green replaced by red and brown
First leaves tumble down
Sun sits low in hazy sky
Swallows southward fly

I Choose a Life of Gratitude

I choose a life of gratitude
Whatever lies in store
I have my health, a little wealth
What could I ask for more?

My heart is filled with love for life
Sees beauty everywhere
My friend if you, are feeling blue
I've so much love to spare

With zest and zeal, I'll gladly take
Each opportunity
And this my vow, before you now
To live courageously

I will not let life pass me by
I'll treasure every minute
Each day I will appreciate
The beauty that's within it

When troubles come, I won't give up
But always persevere
Knowing they will strengthen me,
I'll face them without fear

I'll focus on the things I love
Ignore regrets and strife
And endless positivity
Will be my way of life

I do not live in ignorance
I know I will face sorrow
When dark days come I'll focus on
A brighter day tomorrow

I have so much to celebrate
There's goodness to be found
I count my blessings daily
And I find that they abound

I choose a life of gratitude
The choice is mine to make
Not for the happiness it brings
Nor for good karmas' sake

For one day, when the time will come
To lay this life aside
I'll know I lived it to the full
My choices justified.

15.9.24

A child is born and gently lies
In loving arms that soothe his cries
With wonder, opens gazing eyes
Welcome to this world

So unprepared for what's ahead
And yet, you feel no sense of dread
But rest in blissful peace instead
Welcome to this world

A heart that's filled with truth alone
All darker thoughts remain unknown
Reflection of the love you're shown
Welcome to this world

Born to a life that's oh so wild
And yet you lay, so undefiled
Our precious little baby child
Welcome to this world

Haiku #10

And if this mad life
Sees fit to bless you with love
Be thankful, my friend

I Cannot Make It Through the Day

I cannot make it through the day
The clouds are dark, the sky is grey
And nothing seems to go my way
I cannot make it through the day

There is no way that I can see
To live my life courageously
Or find a path that's trouble-free
There is no way that I can see

My tunnel holds no distant light
As I walk through this endless night
No hope of rescue in my sight
My tunnel holds no distant light

I fear this day will be my last
The dice of destiny are cast
All prospect of salvation past
I fear this day will be my last

Or maybe it will not end here
The gloom around my heart might clear
A bright new dawn may soon appear
Yes, maybe I should persevere

What Goes Up...

'What goes up must come down,'
I read this in a book
That's why I'm standing on this spot
With such a hopeful look
I've stood here very patiently
Since half past two today
When I let go of my red balloon
And watched it float away.

Grandad

Grandad was always my hero
Funny, smart, gentle and kind
With a big booming voice
That was never afraid
To share what he had on his mind.

He taught me the things of importance
Not fancy cars, houses or wealth
But family, friendship
A true love of life,
Happiness, humour and health.

Sometimes he'd come to collect us from school
We'd all happily amble along
And I'll never forget
How he'd cheerfully sing
The words to his 'rainy day' song.

Grandad found joy in his garden
Growing beautiful flowers and more
He'd be found in his greenhouse
Surrounded by plant pots
Dahlias and roses galore.

If ever you went to a local boot sale
You might well bump into our 'Grandy'
For he loved finding bargains
Almost as much
As he loved a cream tea or a shandy.

Grandad passed on early this year
Just before he would turn 93
I stood by his side
As he peacefully passed
Surrounded by family.

Grandad, you won't be forgotten
For you in our hearts, there will always be room
And we'll think of you often
Remembering your smile
Whenever the dahlias bloom.

Ode to a Gammon Joint

I bought a tasty gammon joint
The best one in the store
I didn't pay too much for it
Just three pound sixty-four

I drove home to my kitchenette
Took out my trusty pan
Waited thirty minutes then
With gusto, I began

I covered it with apple juice
Chopped up some herbs and spices
Added in some garlic cloves
A couple lemon slices

Drizzled it with honey
Placed some onion on the side
Topped it with a bay leaf:
My gammon glorified!

I switched my crockpot on to low
And left it gently cooking
But after just an hour or so
I couldn't help but look in

I raised the lid, the room was filled
With such a heavenly smell
I dipped my finger in the juice
It tasted great as well!

Content, I let it bubble on
The flavours bursting free
Aromas drifting round the house
Quite deliciously

Finally, that joint was done
Boiled to perfection
I placed it on a wooden board
And carved it with affection

I bought a tasty gammon joint
It really was a winner
And now we're all enjoying it
With egg and chips for dinner.

She Spoke to Me

She spoke to me in tender tones
My senses all alerted
For loneliness had been my lot
All other loves deserted.

She smiled and took a closer step
Such beauty marked her face
And gently she engulfed me
With a passionate embrace.

I brushed her lips with mine, aware
One kiss would still my heart
Our gazes locked; we fell as one
Never more to part.

Precariously Stacked (The Book Collector)

Precariously stacked beside his bed
There stand three towers of books unread
And in the living room next door
In boxes, several hundred more.

Each title chosen with great care
From cosy bookshops, here and there
Not realising that their fate
Would be to simply sit and wait.

The stories locked between their covers
Of mystery, intrigue and lovers
Lie waiting just to be awoken
Destined to remain unspoken?

And yet each week, the piles will rise
As new books catch his wandering eyes
For the book collector cannot resist
Adding to his reading list.

His intention when he brings them home
Is reading each and every tome
But time would not allow such pleasure
Thus, they became his untouched treasure.

Some volumes will in time become
A very special chosen one
Selected finally to be read
Their words arising from the dead.

But many chosen do not last
Rejected soon, their moment passed
A page or two, then nothing more
Discarded now forevermore.

Just once in a while, one might survive
When the words in its pages come alive
For there's always a chance the shoe will fit
And a book will draw him into it.

A likeable hero, a gripping first page,
An early enigma designed to engage
A twist in the plot or a colourful setting
The dastardly villain we keep on forgetting.

For those few books, and their writers, so skilled
Their destiny will become fulfilled
For the book collector will ne'er outgrow
A story that has gripped him so.

He'll share that story far and wide
Ensure its tales are magnified
And for that precious book itself
A special place upon a shelf.

Another Cup of Tea

Let's have another cup of tea my dear
For chilly is the air and dark the night
And you will be much safer staying here

Your path has been a troubled one this year
You've stumbled through without an end in sight
Let's have another cup of tea my dear

This night is filled with many things to fear
Inside the fire's burning warm and bright
And you will be much safer staying here

I cannot guarantee to bring you cheer
But I can seek to understand your plight
Let's have another cup of tea my dear

Outside the door there's evil drawing near
But safe within 'tis banished by the light
And you will be much safer staying here

Your weary soul is weakening it's clear
And soon there will remain no strength to fight
Let's have another cup of tea my dear
And you will be much safer staying here

What is Beauty?

"What is beauty?"
The young boy asked
I looked at him and smiled
"It is not something easy to
Explain to you, my child."

I glanced around the room
At all the people sitting there
And realised that each of them
Had truths that they could share.

I turned and asked the question
To the lady by my side
She paused and then responded
So soft and dignified:

"Beauty does not age," she said
"It does not fade away
This ring is just as beautiful
As on my wedding day.

My husband placed it on my hand
Thirty-seven years ago
And with every day that passes by
Its beauty seems to grow."

A lady sitting close to us
With scars across her cheek
Lent a little closer
And began to slowly speak:

"Beauty is not an appearance
For appearances can deceive
And sometimes there are beauties
That the eye cannot perceive.

Yet often things that might appear
Lifeless, dull or plain
Can offer unexpected joy
And bring you life again."

"Beauty is a personal thing,"
A creaking voice declared
The speaker was an older man
Scrawny and grey-haired.

"The things that I find beautiful
To you might not appeal,
For beauty is determined
By how things make us feel."

"It's true!" piped up a second man
"For nature has great beauty too,
I feel a sense of inner peace
When gazing at the sea so blue.

Walking through a forest
Or relaxing by a lake
For there is a kind of beauty that
No man could ever make!"

Just then a nurse stepped through the door
Looked round and said with pride:
"Beauty is a quality
That comes from deep inside.

My mother, she was beautiful,
For all her words were kind
She had an inner beauty
Which is very hard to find."

"Beauty is imperfect,"
Laughed a biker, clad in leather
"For there's something rather beautiful
In how things fit together.

This life can be chaotic
But step back and you might see
Things happen for a reason
And that's beautiful to me!"

Silence fell across the room
The young boy deep in thought
"Thank you for providing me,
The answers that I sought,

I think I understand it now,
For you each have shared a part:
Beauty has depth
And beauty has breadth
And beauty comes from the heart!"

Teary-eyed, as that young boy left
I turned back to my wife
She smiled at me and softly said
"What a beautiful, beautiful life!"

Multiple Perfect Moments

One perfect moment in the sea
The blissful deep surrounding me
As playful waves caress my skin
I feel a well of joy within
A gentle breeze enwraps my mind
Leaving all my woes behind.

One perfect moment in a stream
More heavenly than my wildest dream
Sweet waters washing over me
A blanket of tranquillity
Whist golden sunshine softly glows
Escorting me to blest repose.

One perfect moment, feeling small
Beneath a mighty waterfall
Whose torrents drown all other sounds
While emerald features formed around
Protect my mind from all alarms
Embraced by nature's wildest charms.

One perfect moment 'neath the sky
A warm fire crackling closely by
As we admire the stars so bright
And marvel at the infinite
E'en time itself no more has power
Frozen in this flawless hour.

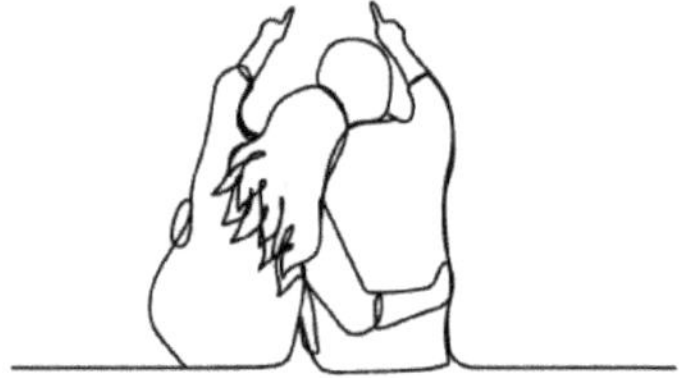

Whodunnit #2

In the slumbering village of Pinkerton Green
The local headteacher is dead
He was found by the caretaker, Bert, who reports
"'E's been battered right over 'is 'ead!"

Upon finding the body, Bert's first course of
action
Was a swig of his brandy, to help him feel fine
Then he plucked up the courage to deal with the
matter
Went to the office and dialled 999.

"All units alert! There's a murder to solve,"
Declared Sergeant Stephens – on duty that day
"And DCI Monks must be called for at once
Somebody fetch him without a delay!"

In no time at all the whole village was flooded
With police cars, forensics and press
A sign on the gate read 'The school will be
closed,
Till we manage to sort out this mess!'

The headteacher's desk was rather chaotic
With folders and documents scattered around
"Perhaps," pondered Stephens "I ought to look
through them,
In case there's some evidence here to be found."

Some performance reviews in a folder marked
'staffing'
A list of the kids who were due in detention
Some rotas, some letters, a couple of sketches
And a poster about a robotics convention.

DCI Monks soon arrived at the school
In his trusty old, rusty old, musty old ford
He was briefed by the sergeant, then turned his
attention
To the facts of the matter that must be explored.

Montgomery Jeffs was the coroner summoned
To enter the crime scene with caution and care
He expertly studied the body before him
And in no time at all, he returned to declare:

"The cause of the death was a blow to the head
Or blunt force trauma, an expert might say
He was struck from behind with a pole of some
kind
And fell in a rather unfortunate way.

Upon falling he suffered a further concussion
And was hit with the weapon several times more
The beating was brutal and caused his demise
But which blow was fatal, it's hard to be sure."

"And the time of the death?" the inspector
inquired,
Jeffs pondered the question before he replied
"I'd hazard a guess around 5:47,
Give or take 30 minutes each side."

Meanwhile Sergeant Stephens had been on the
case
Exercising his excellent skills in detection
He'd found out some info that narrowed the
suspects
From Judith, who worked in reception.

The signing-in system – electronic and new
Gives a record consistent and clear
"At the time of the murder, given what we've
been told
There were just seven people still here.

The headteacher, of course, his secretary,
Maude,
A contractor repairing a fault,
An elderly cleaner and three of the teachers
Miss Gray, Mr. Jones and Miss Gault."

The last one to leave, so the records revealed
Was a teacher named Anabelle Gray
She'd been working quite late laminating
resources
To add to her classroom display.

"I saw nothing unusual," she softly reported
With a smile and a wink and a flick of her hair
"When I walked past his office, the door was
shut tight
I assumed there was nobody there."

"The headteacher was kind – a pleasure to work
for
I simply can't think who would wish him such
harm."
Then she burst into tears (that might not have
been real)
Whilst retaining her feminine charm.

Mr. Jones shared a story remarkedly close
To the one that his colleague Miss Gray had to
tell
He was in the next room the whole of the
evening
Putting displays up as well.

As their rooms were adjacent, they could vouch
for each other
To alleviate any unwanted suspicion
Monks considered this view: was the alibi true,
Or simply a planned coalition?

The elderly cleaner was a lady named Doris
With her hair in a bow and a '50s-style dress
She had stories to tell, a whole lot of memories
And a strong tendency to digress.

She'd worked in the school for at least 40 years
(though for how long she'd stay now she
couldn't be sure)
She's cleaned classrooms for teachers, scrubbed
toilets and hallways
Smiled at thousands of children as they walked
through the door.

The next to be interviewed by the detective
Was Maude, who was traumatized by the events
She stuttered and mumbled through sniffles and
tears
But nothing she said seemed to make any sense.

"Come quickly, Maude, quickly… something to
show you
Don't panic, Maude, panic… everything's fine
The children, the children… it's all for the
children
Not his job, not their job, not your job, not
mine…"

By now the police had tracked down the
contractor
A young electrician, known simply as 'Curt'
He'd returned to the school to help with
enquiries
When he'd heard of the tragedy from his dad,
Bert.

"If yer lookin' fer motive, you can count me
right out, mate,
I've 'ad plenty of work since this guy became
'ead
I was 'elping to teach 'im about electronics,
I'll be out of a bob or two now that he's dead!"

Miss Abigail Gault was the last to be questioned
A fierce and formidable creature
Though her colleagues were useless, and her
class was the worst
She had nothing specific against the headteacher.

She'd heard nothing, done nothing, seen nothing
unusual
"You're wasting your time even talking to me!
I was marking assessments here till six o'clock
When I promptly went home for my tea!"

The detective and Stephens sat down and
perused
All the evidence, statements and clues
Were they anywhere near any kind of solution?
Or was this just a case they were destined to
lose?

Just then an officer burst in the room
"We've been searching all over the place
And have rounded up items that might be the
weapon"
He proclaimed with a triumphant look on his
face.

"The wounds on the headteacher's head are
consistent
With the wounds that these weapons would
make
We've a dusty old broom, a few hockey sticks
A shovel, a mop and a rake."

DCI Monks glanced once more round the room
As he pieced the whole puzzle together
"Gather everyone into the library," he said
For that's how detectives have done it forever.

"As is often the case," the detective began
"This crime was a murder of passion
But not by a lover or a jealous ex-wife
No, this crime came about in a quite different
fashion."

"This headteacher was constantly looking for
ways
To help the school run more efficient and leaner
Here in my hand, you will see he had planned
A design for a robotic cleaner!"

A gasp round the room and a whimper from
Maude
As Doris's elderly face turned quite red
"I did it, is true, with my mop, you'll have
guessed,
And frankly, I'm glad that he's dead!"

"For 40 long years I've worked at this school
Keeping every last inch of it clean
And now I'm sent packing with a pitiful payoff
Replaced by some fancy machine!"

"Well, what's done, is done," she softly
concluded,
Bowed her heard gently, tutted and sighed
Two young policemen helped her into a car
Which took her away to be tried.

As he climbed in his car, the detective felt glad
Case closed – he'd once more been effective
"At least for today, I guess I won't be
Replaced by a robot detective!"

Final Thoughts

With my final breath
Above all, I wish to say
I lived my life well